Last Night I Dreamed of

HORSES

Last night I

dreamed of horses,

and this is what

I saw...

In my dreams

an untamed chestnut stallion

raced across an otherworldly

landscape.

In my dreams
a graceful gray mare trotted through a
mystical land of colossal trees and
dazzling waterfalls.

In my dreams

a gleaming bay stallion jerks

to a halt and turns to me with

an inquisitive stare.

In my dreams
a gentle chestnut mare ambled
through an autumn forest filled with
leaves of gold.

In my dreams
a sweet chestnut foal spent a long, lazy
morning in a lush green pasture.

In my dreams
a gray stallion trotted toward a gloomy
castle, lit by a harvest moon.

In my dreams
a golden palomino crossed a
luminous green pasture with
nimble strides.

In my dreams

a pair of frisky mares pranced

through freshly-fallen snow.

In my dreams

a dappled bay stallion flew across

the dusty earth as twilight storm

clouds gathered.

In my dreams
a placid gray mare paused in the
forest, and time stood still.

In my dreams

a bay stallion trotted

through a golden

grove of trees.

In my dreams
three spirited horses galloped wild and free,
stirring up blinding clouds of dust.

In my dreams
a dappled gray mare basked
in the light of a bright
fallen moon.

In my dreams
a bay stallion walked beneath a brilliant
sun, his coat bathed in golden light.

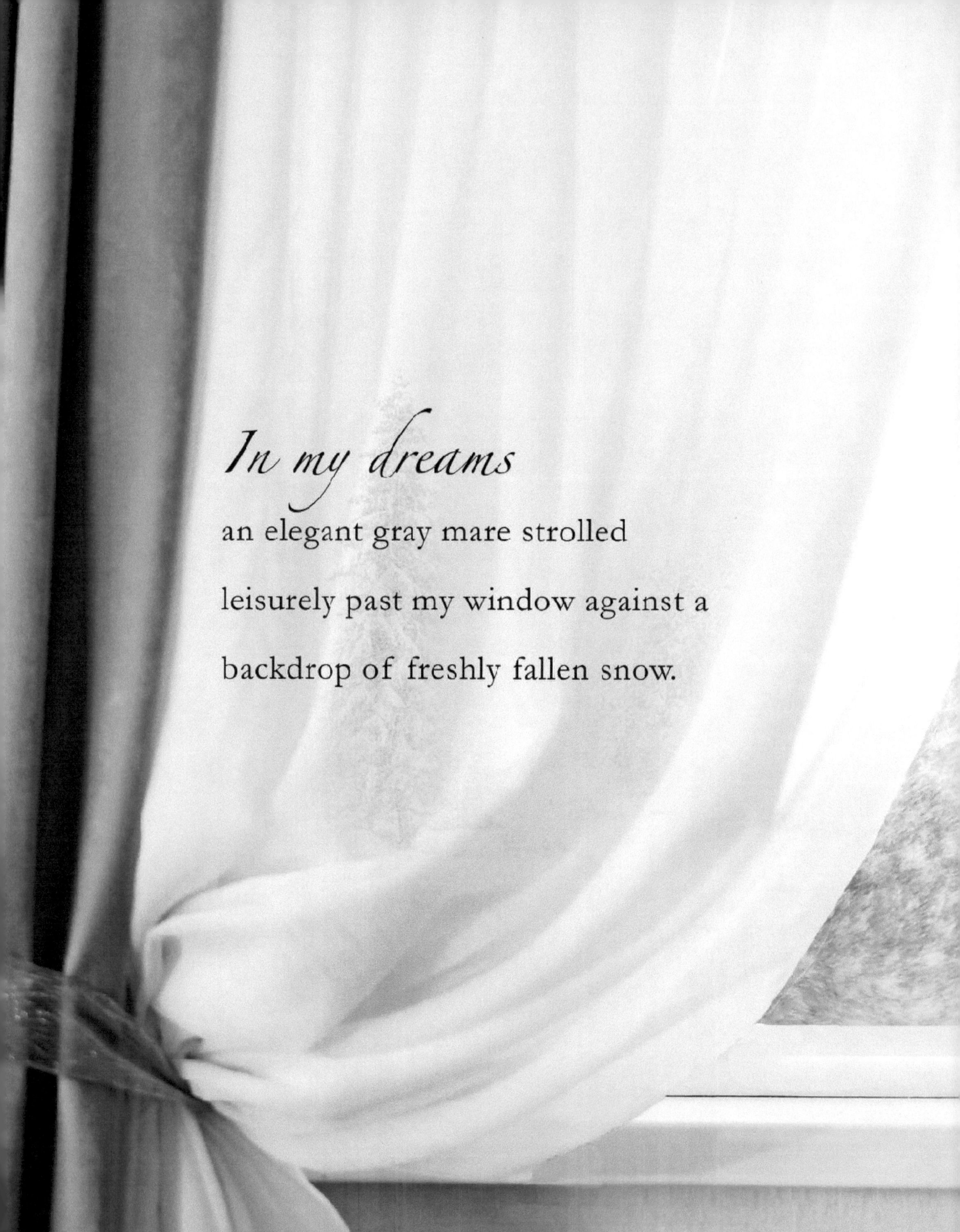

In my dreams
an elegant gray mare strolled
leisurely past my window against a
backdrop of freshly fallen snow.

In my dreams
a white stallion came from
the sea, the tide splashing
against his hooves.

In my dreams

a pretty Arabian mare posed

against a bright morning sky.

In my dreams

a playful filly cavorted in a

field of red poppies.

In my dreams

a lively dun mare leaped from

the pages of an enchanted book

and told me a magical story.

In my dreams
a beautiful gray mare
splashed in the tide along
the ocean's edge.

In my dreams
a gleaming bay mare raced
through the beams of a
brilliant sunset.

In my dreams

a gray mare galloped aloft through

through eternal blue-gray skies.

In my dreams
a majestic black stallion thundered
across the earth beneath a
spectacular sunset.

In my dreams
a pair of carefree horses galloped
in unison across a sunlit field.

In my dreams

a chestnut mare stood poised

and alert, mesmerized by the

misty morning sun.

In my dreams

I'm greeted by a sweet gray

mare beneath a beautiful

flowering tree.

In my dreams
a black stallion raced through a
stormy night, jagged lightning
bolts crashing around him.

In my dreams

a dun stallion danced across

midnight clouds, as if he

was lighter than air.

In my dreams
black and white horses
galloped side by side.

In my dreams
a dark stallion stood
calmly at the edge of
turbulent waters.

In my dreams

a dappled gray mare dashed across a

winter meadow at twilight, pristine snow

flying from beneath her hooves.

When you dream
of horses, which ones
do you see?